Mark H. Hoeksema

Studies in
JAMES

REFORMED
FREE PUBLISHING
ASSOCIATION

Jenison, Michigan

Scripture cited is taken from the Authorized (King James) Version

Reformed Free Publishing Association
1894 Georgetown Center Drive
Jenison MI 49428
616-457-5970
www.rfpa.org
mail@rfpa.org

Book design and typesetting by Erika Kiel

ISBN 978-1-936054-94-7

Introduction

James is the first of the seven general or catholic epistles. That is, James did not write to a particular congregation, but collectively to believers in his day. By way of introduction, various aspects of the epistle should be noted.

The Writer

As is true of all scripture, the author of the book is the Holy Spirit, who inspired James to write what he did and how he did it. In the study of this epistle, therefore, we must regard it as being the infallible, perspicuous, and authoritative word of God.

The writer is James, the half brother of Christ. In the New Testament this name refers to seven different people who shared it. This is understandable, since "James" is the Greek equivalent of the common Hebrew name "Jacob." The writer is not to be confused with James the son of Alpheus, or with James, the brother of John and the son of Zebedee, who was killed by Herod in AD 44, or with any of the others who shared his name. James and his brothers did not believe in his brother Christ during his ministry because of their mistaken idea of the Messiah (John 7:5). Jesus appeared to James personally after the resurrection (1 Cor. 15:7) and James believed at that time. Very early in the history of the New Testament church, James, together with Peter, assumed a position of leadership (Acts 12:17). At the council in Jerusalem, he gave advice regarding the circumcision of the Gentiles, and his advice was followed (Acts 15:13–29).

Although the date of his writing cannot be fixed precisely, most commentators agree that it was about AD 40, only ten years after Christ's death and resurrection.

The Addressees

James writes to the twelve tribes (James 1:1). This should not be understood literally, since the tribes of Israel no longer had definitive and distinctive existence. Rather, it implies that he writes in general to Jewish converts to the Christian church.

James further defines the twelve tribes as those who are scattered abroad. Literally these are the Jews of the *diaspora*, or dispersion. This can be understood in more than one sense.

First, the expression "Jews of the dispersion" refers in a general sense to the nation of Israel that was scattered throughout the known world at the time of the Assyrian and Babylonian captivities, hundreds of years prior to the time of Christ and James. Thousands of Jews could be found in virtually every nation of the extensive Roman empire of James' day. Many, perhaps most, were secular or ethnic Jews only, although many still held to the hope of the Messiah in accordance with God's promise.

Second, following the death and resurrection of Christ, many believed on the Messiah. This made them the objects of persecution on the part of those who rejected him. The center of the church was initially located in Jerusalem, and when the persecution of the believers became increasingly severe there, they fled throughout the regions of Judea and Samaria (Acts 8:1), as well as to Phenice, Cyprus, and Antioch (Acts 11:19).

Third, from the general vicinity of Palestine, the gospel spread to the regions of Galatia, and from there throughout the rest of the Mediterranean world. The members of the early church who fled from Jerusalem and the surrounding area because of persecution soon discovered that opposition followed them wherever they went. The Roman empire ruled the world of that day and did all in its power to destroy the church. The Christians were despised, deprived of their jobs, and robbed of their properties. Some were imprisoned and killed. Besides, the unbelieving Jews, their brethren according to the flesh, bitterly hated and oppressed them. This implies that James writes to the very early believers, who were scattered throughout the world.

James' epistle is unique in scripture in the way that it addresses its readers. He uses widely varying language in addressing them. On the one hand, he rather rudely addresses them as "adulterers and adulteresses" (4:4). On the other hand, he lovingly calls them "my brethren" (1:3 and 2:1) and "my beloved brethren" (1:16). Why he does this should be a subject of discussion.

The Purpose of James

The primary purpose of the book of James is to define the relation between justification and the law.

On the one hand, there were those among the early Jewish converts who were reluctant to continue to keep the Old Testament traditions of works-righteousness in addition to or because of their faith in Christ. Thus James instructs these new converts concerning the correct relation between the keeping of the law and doing good works. Like Paul, he teaches that the keeping of the law is not meritorious, because justification is by faith only. Nevertheless, the works of the law are the evidence and fruit of a living faith.

On the other hand, some in the early church went to the other extreme of antinomianism. They rejected completely the keeping of the law and denied the necessity of doing good works, asserting that doing good works contradicted justification by faith alone. James therefore defines the correct relation between faith and works.

In the context of good works, James admonishes believers as to how they are to live in the world by doing good works as the fruit of justification by faith. He discusses many aspects of how they must conduct themselves, notably regarding the use of the tongue, as well as many other aspects of the Christian life.

Thus James' epistle is very practical.

The Issues

Four main issues regarding the epistle should be addressed and discussed.

First is the apparent contradiction between James and Paul regarding the doctrine of justification. James apparently teaches justification by works. This is the reason that the Roman Catholic Church appeals to this epistle to justify its erroneous doctrine of works-righteousness. Paul teaches the doctrine of justification by faith alone, in direct contradiction to the teaching of Rome. Harmonizing these two ideas is essential to the correct understanding of the truth of justification.

Second, the book is practical in that it addresses various aspects of the Christian life. On the surface it is perhaps the least doctrinal and most practical book in scripture. Some have criticized this apparent lack of balance and express the fear that this practical character then reduces the Christian life to a legalistic list of dos and don'ts. However, more careful study will reveal that his objection is not valid. In making his practical applications, James links them to an attribute or activity of God (1:5, 17; 2:5, 19; 3:9; 4:5–6, 8, 15; 5:11, 15).

Third, most readers want to know the main idea(s) of what they read, and they look for a logical progression of thought. This is difficult to do in James. The epistle seems to consist of loosely connected ideas, and it is hard to grasp the continuity and purpose of what he writes. Yet the book is coherent, both as to its ideas and by means of connecting words, although it is unnecessary to produce a complex structure into which everything must fit. The epistle is the word of God, and it must be accepted and treated as such, whether or not every problem can be solved and all connections perfectly understood.

Fourth, the book has been criticized for its apparent lack of Christ-centeredness. "The Lord Jesus Christ" is mentioned only twice in the epistle, while "God" or "the Lord" are mentioned repeatedly. Perhaps the reason is that James is aware that his predominantly Jewish addressees are more familiar with these names. In any event, there can be no doubt that James' teachings are in harmony with those of his brother Jesus.

The Methodology

This is a study guide, not a commentary. It therefore does not take a statement or an explanation format, but a question format, which is intended to help God's people define and understand James' concepts and terms, as well as their relationships to one another. I have deliberately asked the difficult "why" and "how" questions in order to foster an understanding of this scripture. As much as possible the questions are intentionally leading, interspersed with helpful remarks, with the goal of encouraging discussion and assisting in the understanding of James, whether in Bible study societies or on a personal level. To the extent that the questions are accurately answered in the light of scripture, the student of James will gain an understanding of the epistle.

To help organize the various subjects that James discusses, I have chosen to follow the letter's divisions into sections used almost identically by Kistemaker, Bird, and Tasker.

Study Resources

Herman Hanko, *Faith Made Perfect: Commentary on James*, Reformed Free Publishing Association.

Anthony E. Bird, *Practice Makes Perfect*, EP BOOKS INC. Webster, New York.

Simon Kistemaker, *New Testament Commentary: James, 1–3 John*, Baker Book House.

Robert Johnstone, *A Commentary on James (Geneva Series)*, Banner of Truth Trust.

R. V. G. Tasker, *The General Epistle of James: Introduction and Commentary*, Eerdmans.

James 1:1

Greeting

1. James gives a brief introduction. He calls himself a servant, literally, "a slave."

2. Why does James call himself a slave? What does this term imply?

3. What does it mean that he is a servant "of God and of the Lord Jesus Christ"?

4. Does the term "twelve tribes" have a symbolic meaning (Matt. 19:28; Acts 26:7)? Are we also included in the twelve tribes? If so, in what sense?

5. The word *greeting* comes from the same word family as *joy*. Why does James use this word?

James 1:2–4

Trials and Temptations

1. In verse 2 James speaks of temptations, and in verse 3 of trials or testings. The Greek uses the same word for both, but they are different as to author, purpose or motive, and outcome. In what ways is this true?

2. Is "temptations" the correct translation in verse 2? Why or why not?

3. How are temptations and trials related? How can trials and persecution be temptations? How can temptations be trials?

4. What are divers temptations? What are some that James mentions in this epistle?

5. What does it mean to "fall into" them?

6. Are not the words *joy* and *trials* an oxymoron? How can trials be met with joy?

7. What is the patience (literally: perseverance) mentioned in verses 3 and 4?

8. What does letting "patience have her perfect work" mean? Does perfect mean without sin?

9. Verse 4 literally speaks of being "mature and complete." What does this mean?

James 1:5–8

Obtaining Wisdom

1. James moves from "lacking nothing" in verse 4 to "if you lack" in verse 5. Is this a contradiction?

2. What is wisdom (Prov. 2:6)? How are knowledge and wisdom related? Can a person have knowledge without wisdom or vice versa?

3. In what respect can we lack wisdom?

4. What is the solution to a lack of wisdom (v. 5)?

5. "Upbraideth not" is literally "without finding fault" (v. 5). What does it mean that God gives without finding fault?

6. How must we ask God for wisdom (v. 6)?

7. If we waver ("doubt"), what will be the result (v. 6)?

8. How would you describe a man who is double minded ("two-souled") (v. 8)?

9. What is the resulting instability?

James 1:9–11

Rejoicing in Poverty and Wealth

1. James draws a contrast between the poor ("low degree" or "humble circumstances") and the rich. Although both are members of the church, why does he refer to the poor man as a "brother," but does not do this regarding the rich (vv. 9–10)?

2. James is not concerned with riches, but with those who possess riches. Are riches wrong in themselves? What does Jesus say about the rich in Matthew 19:23?

3. The brother of low degree is admonished to rejoice or take pride in the fact that he is exalted (v. 9). What does this mean? How should he do this?

4. In what sense must the rich man rejoice in that he is made low? What reason does James give for doing this (v. 10)?

5. Under what analogy does James write concerning the brevity of life (v. 11)?

6. Why is it important for the rich to remember the brevity of life?

James 1:12–15

Trials and Temptations—Again

1. James returns to the subject of trials (testings) and temptations about which he has spoken previously. Since the Greek uses the same word for both, which word is meant in verse 12?

2. In what sense is the word used in verse 13?

3. What does it mean to endure?

4. Of what does the "crown of life" consist? Who receives it? What is the relation between enduring temptations and receiving the crown of life (v. 12)?

5. Why does James give the admonition of verse 13?

6. Why is it wrong to say that God is the author of temptation?

7. What is the source of temptations (v. 14)?

8. In verse 15 James implies the figure of pregnancy and giving birth. How does lust bring forth sin?

9. How does sin bring forth death?

James 1:16–18

Perfect Gifts

1. Why does James admonish his readers not to err ("be deceived") (v. 16)?

2. In what sense are God's gifts good and perfect (v. 17)?

3. What attribute of God is described in the last part of verse 17?

4. What is the first work of the Father of lights in the hearts of the elect sinner (v. 18)?

5. What word in verse 18 indicates this truth?

6. What is God's will? In his choosing of his people, what truth is implied?

7. What truth is meant by "begat he us" (v. 18)?

8. "That we should be a kind of firstfruits" is the purpose of regeneration. The reference is to the Old Testament feast of firstfruits. What is the meaning of "firstfruits"? How are God's people firstfruits?

James 1:19–21

Receiving the Word

1. James introduces a new subject by "wherefore" and by calling his readers his "beloved brethren." Of what truth is "wherefore" a consequence or conclusion?

2. James gives three admonitions in verse 19: be quick to hear, slow to speak, and slow to anger. What does it mean to be quick to hear? Why is it important to be quick to hear?

3. Why is it necessary to be slow to speak?

4. We must be slow to anger. Why? What is meant by the righteousness of God? How does one work the righteousness of God? How does wrath fail to work the righteousness of God?

5. "Wherefore" in verse 21 indicates the conclusion that must be drawn from verse 20. What is the filthiness from which we must rid ourselves?

6. What is "superfluity of naughtiness" ("a superabundance of evil")?

7. What is "the word"? What does it mean that the word is engrafted or planted in us?

8. What does it mean to accept the word? In what manner are we to do this?

9. How does the implanted word save our souls?

James 1:22–25

Hearers and Doers

1. Speaking of the engrafted word, James admonishes his readers to be not merely listeners of that word, but also to do what the word says. If we are only hearers, what is the result (v. 22)?

2. The word hearers is related to the word disobedience. What does this tell us? How do we deceive ourselves by being hearers only?

3. James compares the hearer to one who beholds his natural face in a mirror (v. 24). In his day mirrors were made of polished metal, not of glass, and the reflection was imperfect. What does this figure tell us about hearing the word?

4. What is the result of the hearer who listens to the word but does not do it (v. 24)?

5. Continuing the figure of a mirror, James describes the doer of the word. What does it mean to be a doer of the law (v. 25)?

6. What is the law of liberty (literally, "the law that gives freedom") (v. 25)?

7. Why is this law called "perfect" (v. 25)?

8. What does it mean to continue in this law? Why is this necessary (v. 25)?

9. The result is that the doer is blessed. What does it mean to be blessed?

James 1:26–27

Practical Religion

1. James continues his theme of being doers of the word by using the word religion. What does he mean by this term?

2. He also introduces another idea, that of the tongue, about which he will write more later. What does it mean to bridle the tongue (v. 26)?

3. If one does not keep a tight rein on his tongue, he deceives his heart. What does it mean to deceive one's heart (v. 26)?

4. Therefore his religion is vain. What does *vain* mean?

5. Why does James choose the tongue (among other possible sins) as that which makes one's religion vain?

6. James positively defines pure and undefiled (faultless) religion in verse 27 in terms of what God and the Father accepts. Why is God called "the Father"? What is his connection between the widows and orphans?

7. In what sense are the widows and orphans distressed?

8. What does it mean to keep oneself unspotted from the world? How is this connected with caring for the widows and orphans (v. 27)?

James 2:1–4

Respect of Persons

1. James begins another section of his letter by addressing his readers as "my brethren." He tells them not to have the faith of the Lord Jesus Christ, the Lord of glory, with respect of persons.

2. What is the meaning of faith here? Is it objective or subjective?

3. Why does he call Jesus Christ "the Lord of glory" (v. 1)?

4. What is the connection between showing favoritism and having faith in Christ?

5. Respect of persons is literally "to receive the face." What does this mean?

6. What illustration of favoritism does James give in verses 2 and 3?

7. Is this illustration hypothetical or factual?

8. Why would people in the church honor a rich man and despise a poor man?

9. In what ways can we be guilty of showing favoritism?

10. What does the term *partial* indicate (v. 4)?

11. What does it mean to be judges with (not of) evil thoughts? What effect does this have on judgment?

James 2:5-7

Poor and Rich

1. Continuing his discussion of respect of persons, James asks a rhetorical question in verse 5. Why does he address his readers as "beloved brethren"?

2. To what truth does God's choosing refer (v. 5)?

3. In what sense are the chosen poor? In what way are they rich?

4. Why does God choose the poor and not the rich?

5. What is God's kingdom? Who will inherit it (v. 5)?

6. Whom is James addressing in verse 6?

7. How did the rich oppress or exploit the poor (v. 6)?

8. Why would the rich drag the poor into the courts of the land?

9. What is it to blaspheme? What is the worthy name by which they were called? How did they blaspheme that name (v. 7)?

James 2:8–11

Keeping the Royal Law

1. James shows that respect of persons breaks the law. To what part of the law does he refer?

2. How does showing favoritism break the law?

3. Why does James describe the law as "royal"? What does this mean (v. 8)?

4. How does James show the seriousness of breaking the law (v. 10)?

5. How does James show that the law is a unity (v. 11)?

James 2:12–13

Showing Mercy

1. James admonished his readers to speak and to act as those who will be judged by the law of liberty. What is the law of liberty? How will we be judged by it (v. 12)?

2. What is the mercy of which he speaks in verse 13?

3. What is the judgment of which James speaks (v. 13)?

4. Are mercy and judgment oppositional or contradictory ideas? Why or why not?

5. What parables teach the idea of judgment without mercy?

6. Is the mercy of the last part of verse 13 a divine or a human mercy?

7. What does it mean that mercy rejoices against ("triumphs over") judgment (v. 13)?

James 2:14–17

Faith without Works

1. In the remainder of chapter 2 James deals with the relation between faith and works (deeds). What is the implied answer to the two questions of verse 14?

2. Why does James describe the man of verse 14 as one who *says* or *claims* to have faith?

3. What is the profit or good of which James writes?

4. What example does James use in verses 15–16 regarding faith and works?

5. What is a dead faith? In contrast, what is true faith?

6. What does it mean that faith without works is dead? What does it mean that this faith is "alone" (v. 17)?

James 2:18–19

The Relation of Faith and Works

1. Objections to the truth are common. Who is the "man" who objects in verse 18?

2. Who is the one who has faith? Who is the one who has works (deeds)?

3. Is the one who speaks in verse 18 a hypothetical objector, or is it James?

4. What is the double challenge of verse 18?

5. What does it mean to show one's faith by his works (v. 18)?

6. Whom is James addressing in verse 19?

7. What is James' point in speaking of the devils who tremble before the one God?

James 2:20–24

Justification and Faith

1. James asks three successive rhetorical questions in verses 20–22 to make his point. Whom is James addressing when he speaks to the vain (foolish) man in verse 20?

2. Verse 20 is the heart of James' teaching about faith and works. What is a dead or useless faith? What is true faith?

3. James speaks of justification (v. 21). What is justification?

4. Paul teaches justification by faith alone (Rom. 3:20, 28). James teaches justification by works (v. 21). Do they contradict one another?

5. Do Paul and James speak of justification in two different senses? If so, what are they?

6. How can it be said that Abraham (the example of faith) was justified by works in his offering of Isaac?

7. What is James' solution to the problem of faith vs. works (v. 22)?

8. James uses the example of Abraham. Why?

9. What does it mean that his faith was imputed to him for righteousness (v. 23)?

10. Why does James add that Abraham was called the friend of God (v. 23)?

11. In what way is a man justified by works and not only by faith (v. 24)?

James 2:25–26

The Example of Rahab and Conclusion

1. In verse 25 James uses the example of Rahab. Why does he choose Rahab instead of someone like Abraham?

2. Why is she called "the harlot" here and elsewhere in scripture?

3. How was Rahab justified by works?

4. How is faith related to her justification?

5. What is the meaning of "spirit" as James uses the term in verse 26?

6. What is the meaning of the analogy of verse 26?

James 3:1–2

The Responsibility of Teaching

1. By the use of "My brethren" James begins a new subject. What is the connection between 2:26 and 3:1?

2. James says, "Not many of you should be teachers" (v. 1). What kind of teacher does he have in mind?

3. What reason does James give for his admonition? Does Jesus teach this truth?

4. Why will teachers be judged more strictly than others?

5. What does it mean that we all stumble or err in many ways? What are some of them (v. 2)?

6. What is the significance of "we" in verse 2?

7. Why does James single out not offending in word (v. 2)?

8. Does James teach that we can become sinless by not offending in word?

9. What is the meaning of "the whole body" (v. 2)?

James 3:3-8

The Disproportionate Tongue

1. What three examples of the power of the tongue does James use in verses 3–6?

2. What is the point of comparison of these examples with the tongue (v. 5)?

3. In what way does the tongue boast of great things?

4. What does it mean that the tongue is a fire (v. 6)?

5. What does James mean by "a world of iniquity" or evil (v. 6)?

6. How does the tongue defile or corrupt the whole body (person)?

7. "The course of nature" is literally "the wheel of existence." What does this mean?

8. The word "hell" (v. 6) is more correctly "Gehenna." What is Gehenna? Is Gehenna connected with Satan?

9. What illustrations can be given regarding the ability of man to tame all kinds of creatures (v. 7)?

10. In contrast, what does it mean that the tongue is unruly ("restless") and is full of deadly poison (v. 8)?

James 3:9–12

Praising and Cursing—An Oxymoron

1. We use our tongues to bless (praise) God our Father. Why do we and must we do this? How do we do this?

2. With the same tongue we curse men, who are made after the similitude (likeness) of God. What is the connection between blessing and cursing (v. 10)?

3. Why is it a great sin to use the tongue to curse men?

4. What examples does James use to illustrate this oxymoron of blessing and cursing (vv. 11–12)?

5. What is the point of these examples?

James 3:13–16

Earthly Wisdom

1. James asks a question in verse 13: "Who is wise and understanding among you?" What is wisdom? What is understanding?

2. James' answer is that such a person must show his works out of a good conversation. What is our conversation?

3. Why is meekness (humility) an essential component of doing this?

4. James speaks of earthly wisdom in terms of bitter envying (v. 14). What is bitter envying?

5. Strife is selfish ambition. How does this contradict true wisdom?

6. How do we lie not or deny the truth (v. 14)?

7. False wisdom does not come from heaven, but is earthly, sensual, and devilish (v. 15). What do these three terms mean?

8. What are the confusion and every evil work that are the result of envy and strife (v. 16)?

James 3:17–18

True Wisdom

1. What is wisdom from above? Who is the source of this wisdom (v. 17)?

2. True wisdom has many characteristics. What do these descriptions mean: pure, peace-loving, considerate, submissive, full of mercy and good fruit, impartial and sincere?

3. Who are the peacemakers of whom James speaks in verse 18? What do they do?

4. What is the fruit (harvest) of righteousness?

James 4:1–3

Wars and Fightings

1. James continues the idea of conflict that he began in chapter 3, verses 14 and 16, speaking of wars and fightings. What sort of quarrels and conflicts could he have in mind? Where do they take place?

2. He answers his own question rhetorically: "Do they not come from your own lusts?" What is the meaning of lusts?

3. What does James mean by members (v. 1)? What does it mean that lusts battle within these members?

4. Are the lusts or desires sinful, seeing that those to whom he writes do not receive what they want (v. 2)?

5. Is the killing in verse 2 literal or figurative? In what way do they kill?

6. What is the sin of coveting (desiring to have)?

7. Why do they not receive what they want (v. 2)?

8. If they do ask, they still do not receive. Why not (v. 3)?

9. What is it to consume it upon their lusts (pleasures)?

James 4:4–6

Friends with the World

1. James addresses his readers as "Ye adulteresses" ("adulterers" is not found in the Greek) (v. 4). He uses the term figuratively. What is the meaning of spiritual adultery in scripture, especially in the Old Testament? What truth is violated by such adultery?

2. What is the meaning of "world" as James uses it here (v. 4)?

3. What is it to be friends with the world?

4. What is enmity with God?

5. Who is an enemy of God? What is his fate?

6. James quotes scripture twice to make his point. Is there a specific scripture reference for his first quotation (v. 5)? How are we to understand this quotation?

7. Does the spirit of verse 5 refer to the Holy Spirit or to our spirit?

8. How does the spirit in us lust to envy?

9. God gives more grace (v. 6). To what purpose does he do this?

10. What is the scripture that James quotes in verse 6?

11. What does it mean that God resists or opposes the proud? Who are the proud?

12. What is the grace that he gives to the humble? Who are they?

James 4:7–10

The Remedy for Worldliness

1. By means of several short, sharp admonitions James draws conclusions from what he has just written regarding friendship with the world and enmity against God. He gives practical instruction how to live the Christian life.

2. What is it to submit ourselves to God (v. 7)? How do we do this?

3. How do we resist the devil? How will this resisting result in the devil's fleeing from us?

4. Is God's drawing near to us conditioned by our drawing near to him? What is the relation between these two "drawings"?

5. Especially in an Old Testament context, what is the significance of washing one's hands (v. 8)?

6. Who are the double-minded (v. 8)? How must they cleanse their hearts?

7. James tells his readers to grieve, mourn, and wail (v. 9). Why?

8. Why must laughter be turned to mourning and joy to gloom?

9. What does it mean to humble ourselves (v. 10)?

10. What is the consequence of doing so?

James 4:11–12

Judging the Brother

1. James admonishes his readers not to speak evil of (literally, "slander") one another (v. 11). What does it mean to slander?

2. He directs his admonition to "brethren" (v. 11). In this context, what is the significance of this address?

3. What does it mean to judge the brother?

4. What is the law in these verses?

5. How does one speak against and judge the law?

6. How does the one lawgiver (God) save and destroy?

7. What is James' conclusion (v. 12)? What sin is committed by the one described in these verses?

James 4:13–17

The Will of God

1. In these verses James applies the sin of pride that he implied in verse 12 to the carrying out of business. He begins with the strong expression, "Now listen!" Why does he make such an emphatic point?

2. What attribute of God are those who take the attitude described in verse 13 ignoring?

3. What work of God do they forget or deny?

4. What is James' point in the analogy of verse 14?

5. What is the Lord's will?

6. What do they do in contrast to what they should do?

7. One sins who knows what is right but does not do it (v. 17). Does this mean that ignorance is an excuse? If not, what does this mean?

James 5:1–3

The Perils of Riches

1. James calls emphatic attention to what he is about to say (literally, "Now listen!"). Who are the rich whom he addresses? Are they in the church or outside of it?

2. What three marks of worldly riches does James mention (vv. 2–3)? How are these marks evident today?

3. What does James tell the rich to do (v. 1)? Why?

4. What are the miseries that will come upon the rich?

5. What specific miseries will they suffer? Why are these so serious for the rich?

6. How will the corrosion of their gold and silver testify against them?

7. What are the last days? How do the rich behave regarding them (v. 3)?

James 5:4–6

The Sins of the Rich

1. The rich pile sin upon sin (v. 4). How do they acquire their wealth?

2. In what sense do the unpaid wages cry against the rich?

3. What is the meaning of the Lord's name *Sabaoth*?

4. What is pleasure (v. 5)? What does it mean to be wanton?

5. What figure does James use in verse 5 to describe both the activity and the end of the rich?

6. What does "condemned" imply (v. 6)?

7. Is the murder of verse 6 literal or figurative?

8. What makes the actions of the rich even more sinful?

James 5:7–9

Patience

1. James addresses his "brethren" who are the victims of the rich by counseling patience. What is the patience of which he speaks three times in these verses?

2. Why does James admonish patience (v. 7)?

3. Why does James speak of the coming of the Lord (v. 7)?

4. What illustration does James use to make his point? What are the early and latter rains (v. 7)?

5. What does it mean to stablish your hearts (v. 8)?

6. In what sense is the coming of the Lord near? How is this the reason for patience and standing firm (v. 8)?

7. What is it to grudge against one another? Why must we not do this? What will be the consequence if we do (v. 9)?

James 5:10–11

Examples

1. James assumes the knowledge of the Old Testament by his readers. How are the prophets an example of patience in suffering (v. 10)?

2. How and why did the prophets suffer?

3. How did they show patience?

4. What does it mean that we count the prophets who have persevered "happy" (v. 11)?

5. What was the patience or perseverance of Job? What is the end of the Lord (v. 11)?

6. What is the point of these two examples?

James 5:12

Swearing

1. There is little obvious connection with the context in these words. Yet James sees the matter of the oath as important, for he says "Above all."

2. What does it mean to swear an oath?

3. The Jews were noteworthy for swearing oaths at the slightest provocation. Does James forbid the swearing of all oaths?

4. If swearing was permitted by the Old Testament law, why does James say, "Do not swear"?

5. Under what circumstances are oaths allowable?

6. What is the consequence of improper oaths?

James 5:13–15

The Prayer of Faith

1. James turns to the subject of prayer. In verse 13 he mentions two opposites.

2. What does it mean to be afflicted? Is this physical or spiritual?

3. What should the happy do (v. 13)? Why?

4. Who are the sick of verse 14? Is this sickness physical or spiritual? Or both?

5. Can the elders cure such sickness?

6. What is the significance of the anointing with oil (v. 14)? Does this cure sickness?

7. Does calling on the name of the Lord cure illness?

8. Will the prayer offered in faith always make a sick person well? What if the person dies?

9. What is the connection between healing by the prayer of faith and the forgiveness of sins (v. 16)?

James 5:16–18

The Power of Prayer

1. James continues the subject of prayer from the viewpoint of its power.

2. Why must we confess our sins to one another? Why not to God? Or are both meant (v. 16)?

3. What should be the content of our prayer for one another (v. 16)?

4. In what way are we healed?

5. Does James teach in verse 16 that prayer changes things if we are persistent?

6. In what way is the prayer of the righteous powerful and effective?

7. James uses the example of Elijah. Why does he say that Elijah was a man just like us (v. 17)?

8. The facts of Elijah's prayers are well-known. What is the meaning and point of this example?

9. Why was Elijah's prayer heard?

James 5:19–20

The Conversion of the Sinner

1. James introduces his last subject by the now-familiar term *Brethren*. He presents the situation of one who errs from the truth. What is the truth? What is it to err from that truth (v. 19)?

2. What does it mean to convert?

3. Is it possible for us to convert or bring back a sinner from his evil way? Why or why not?

4. What is the death of which James writes (v. 20)?

5. What does it mean to hide a multitude of sins? How is this the result of conversion (v. 20)?

Notes

Notes

Notes

Notes

www.ingramcontent.com/pod-product-compliance
Lightning Source LLC
Chambersburg PA
CBHW071123260325
24109CB00031B/408